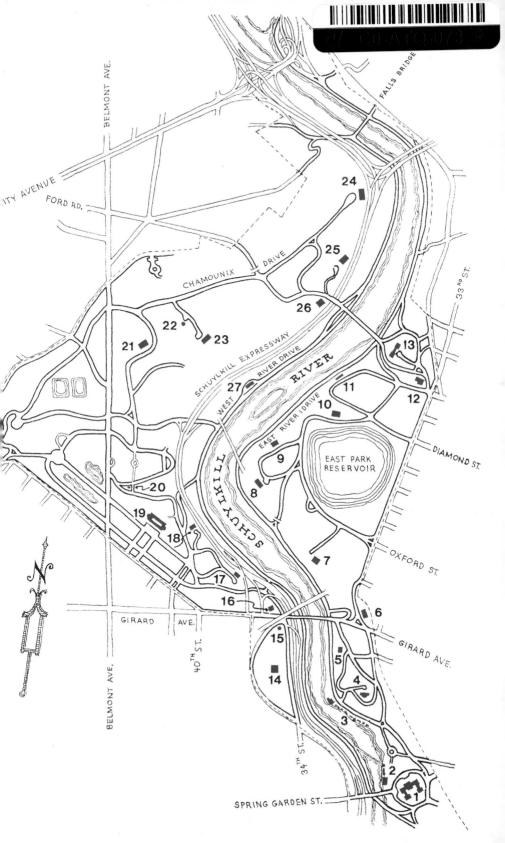

Lights
Along The Schuylkill

BY

MARION W. RIVINUS

DEDICATED TO

MY GREAT GRANDFATHER,

ELI K. PRICE
one of the original Park Commissioners,

MY UNCLE,

ELI KIRK PRICE, JR.
Vice-President of the Park Commission, 1912-1933,

AND

MY COUSIN,

PHILIP PRICE
Vice-President of the Park Commission.

ACKNOWLEDGMENTS

I wish to acknowledge, with grateful thanks, the ready cooperation of the following:

Mr. Philip Price, Vice-President of the Fairmount Park Commission.

The Staff of the Park Commission in City Hall.

Mr. William H. Noble, Jr., former Director of the Park.

Messrs. John B. Kelly, Jr., William J. Cochrane, W. E. Garrett Gilmore of the Schuylkill Navy.

Mr. Martin P. Snyder, Trustee of the Woodford Estate.

Mrs. Henry T. MacNeill and Mr. Stephen MacNeill of the Stephen Moylan Press.

Mrs. Samuel McCreery, President of the Sedgley Club.

Mrs. John S. Gates, Chairman of the Park House Tours, and last, but far from least,

Mrs. Philip A. Brégy, of the Women's Committee of the Philadelphia Museum of Art, who patiently assisted me in checking the galley proofs.

Contents

ADDENDUM #1

ADDENDUM #2

Illustrations

HISTORY OF FAIRMOUNT PARK

I N JUNE, 1812, the City of Philadelphia acquired five acres of
Morris Hill tract designated on old maps as "Faire Mount," as
a site for the municipal water works and a large reservoir.

This was the area now occupied by the Aquarium and the
Art Museum.

Over a period of years more adjacent land was purchased
primarily to protect the water supply so that by 1828 the City
owned some twenty-eight acres, which was specified as a public
park.

In 1844 Lemon Hill and the intervening land were added. In
1856 the estate of Sedgely, somewhat to the north of Lemon Hill,
became City property and ten years later a major acquisition was
made by the purchase of the Lansdowne Estate, home of Governor
John Penn. This was the first property acquired on the west side of
the Schuylkill River and contained 140 acres. In 1868 Jesse and
Rebecca George presented George's Hill to the City, consisting of
about fifty-eight acres.

Since then the additions to Fairmount Park have grown to
include the Wissahickon Gorge, and numerous other localities, so
that today the Fairmount Park Commission has jurisdiction over
some 7,730.887 acres.

Fairmount Park proper consists of about 4,000 acres with the
water area of the Schuylkill River, within the Park, of 379 acres.[1]

Fairmount Park is the largest municipal park in the world.

In the early 1700's and until the dam was built in 1822 the
hills of the Schuylkill were the most desirable residential environs
of the City and many handsome houses with surrounding plantations were erected. The dam stopped the ebb and flow of the tide
which ran up as far as the Falls. The water was backed up, making
marshland of the banks bordering the river, and creating a happy

1-See page 83

I

hunting ground for mosquitoes. This in turn made life in the area very unhealthy and gradually the owners of the beautiful estates were forced to desert them.

Due to the vision of some of our forefathers several of the mansions have been preserved and restored and under the management of the Park Commission present a unique treasure history of our Colonial times in architecture as well as the picture of gracious living.

FAIRMOUNT PARK COMMISSION

The Fairmount Park Commission was created in 1867 to administer the Park and is composed of ten citizens appointed for five-year terms by the Board of Judges of the Court of Common Pleas, and six ex-officio members from the City Government. Among the original commissioners by virtue of their office were:

MORTON McMICHAEL, 1867 – 1869
JOSHUA SPERING, 1867 – 1868
JOSEPH F. MARCER, 1867 – 1870
JOHNATHAN PUGH, 1868 – 1875
FREDERICK GRAFF, 1867 – 1873
STRICKLAND KNEASS, 1867 – 1872

Appointed by the Courts:

ELI K. PRICE, 1867 – 1884
JOHN L. WELSH, 1867 – 1886
WILLIAM SELLERS, 1867 – 1877
JOSEPH HARRISON, 1867 – 1873
JOHN C. CRESSON, 1867 – 1868
N. B. BROWNE, 1867 – 1871
THEODORE CUYLER, 1867 – 1876
HENRY M. PHILLIPS, 1867 – 1884
GUSTAVUS REMAK, 1867 – 1886
GEORGE G. MEADE, 1867 – 1876

LIFE ON THE HILLS OF THE SCHUYLKILL

IN THE earliest days of Philadelphia, Thomas Holmes' original plan made in 1682 called for a High Street (now Market) running from the Delaware to the Schuylkill Rivers, and Penn sold many of the lots on the banks of the Schuylkill "almost as dear as those on the banks of the Delaware." A few houses were actually built there, mostly on small farms, but the whole area was a vast wilderness of thick forest with only a few Indian trails, and too far from the main town to be popular. Gradually the inhabitants moved back to more settled surroundings, but many were careful enough to retain their titles as an investment.

It was not until the country became more opened up and accessible that the prosperous merchant Princes of the city, now arrived at a more gracious style of living, decided to escape from the summer heat, and the Hills of the Schuylkill came into their own. Between 1708 and until the dam was built in 1822 the Hills were the most desirable residential part of Philadelphia, and the early owners of the land, who had the foresight to retain possession, did very well by themselves.

The Country Seats established on the Schuylkill were quite distinct from the plantations of the south, and the Hudson River manors. In the first place the Philadelphians only considered their estates as pleasure abodes during the summer months and practically daily rode back and forth to the city to transact their business, pleasure, or hear the gossip of the day, while their ladies travelled in carriages to attend the assemblies and other parties or for shopping and the theatre.

The near proximity to the City made a vast difference from the plantations and manors which were separated from their nearest city by long distances. Thus a journey to Williamsburg or New York was an event.

The mansions on the Schuylkill were close enough for frequent neighborly intercourse as well. Visiting could be accomplished by road or by private boat and the river could be crossed by fords and ferries, more of which anon.

To add to the amenities there were two fashionable social fishing clubs, the Fort St. Davids and the Schuylkill Fishing Company of the Colony in Schuylkill, which are described in more detail later in this book. Life was gay and cultured, but not frivolous.

Most of the men, besides their great shipping interests in all parts of the world (Philadelphia was then the leading seaport of the Colonies), were active in civic affairs, with a knowledge of the law, many becoming judges, and the ladies had great domestic responsibilities managing large households with constant entertaining and bringing up their children. A gracious hostess was fluent in French, music, and dancing with other accomplishments. She also had to be familiar with the concocting of herbs to preserve the health of her little community. There were no corner drug stores.

Philadelphia was an international metropolis with contacts all over the world, resulting in much foreign culture and tastes. Frequent important travellers arrived, all of whom were welcomed and entertained at these homes, occupied by the leading citizens. To quote Sydney George Fisher, "Probably in no other place on the continent was the love of bright colors and extravagance in dress carried to such extremes. Large numbers of the Quakers yielded to it, and even the very strict ones carried gold-headed canes, gold snuff boxes, and wore great silver buttons on their drab coats and handsome buckles on their shoes. Women were resplendent in silks, satins, velvets, and brocades, and they piled their hair mountains high. It often required hours for the public dresser to arrange one of these headdresses, built up with all manner of stiffening substances and worked into extraordinary shapes."

These contraptions were expected to last for at least a week and between the "stiffening substances," powder, and pomatum, not to mention perspiration, ladies' heads had a tendency to itch. To relieve this discomfort they scratched with long silver sticks,

4

frequently mistaken in more modern times for hat pins by purchasers in antique shops.

The men were not to be left behind in their hair-do affair. Most of them wore wigs of which there was a great variety. There was the "tie-wig," "bag-wig," "nightcap wig," "riding wig," etc., and they usually selected one for a ball or formal occasion on which they did not dare put a hat with its gold lace and trimmings, hence the style of carrying said hat under the arm. They too dressed in velvets and brocades with kneebreeches and some non-Quakers sported a small rapier at parties.

A tailor advertised in 1773, "scarlet, buff, blue, green, crimson, white, skye blue, and other colored superfine cloths."

The judges, which would include our Hill folk, wore on the bench scarlet robes faced with black and long curled, powdered wigs.

The streets of Philadelphia must have been a colorful sight with these gentlemen and ladies interspersed with Indians, sailors, pirates, of which the City had her share, Negro slaves and immigrants, all in their native costumes. Markets were excellent and French cooks and caterers plentiful, foreign delicacies and spices were easily procured, due to the great importing merchants.

Slaves and constantly arriving indentured servants furnished the labor.

Private dinner parties and entertainments were continual, often accompanied by music, performed by the host and his family.

Madeira, ale and punch were the prevailing drinks, and a handsome punch bowl was part of every genteel house equipment, kept near the front door to welcome the arriving or speed the parting guest.

There was much tea drinking amongst the ladies, and it was the custom after an assembly for the gentleman to partake of this beverage with his dancing partner of the evening before.

Fox hunting, fishing, fowling, cock-fighting, and skating were popular masculine sports, while horse racing in the public streets (hence the present Race Street) and around Center Square, now occupied by the City Hall, were the occasions for much extra entertaining. A gentleman's mount was a pacing horse, running and trotting horses were considered only for the vulgar classes.

When the rich merchant Princes began to occupy their country seats on the Hills of the Schuylkill, there were house parties, boating on the River and picnics. It was a happy, interesting life. With their international contacts, culture, and affluence, the Hillers surrounded themselves on their beautiful estates with all the tasteful amenities of life. Formal gardens encompassed the mansions, and the houses were filled with fine tapestries, rugs, hangings, books, furniture, and works of art. Their farms furnished fresh and even exotic fruits and vegetables, meat and other produce; while spices, wines, and other imports came up the Delaware in their ships.

Gay and active as it all sounded, times were growing more tense. Ever since the Stamp Act, colonial feelings were becoming more bitter.

Finally the first Continental Congress was called in Philadelphia to see if these problems could be solved. As the delegates from the other states arrived, they were welcomed by the leading Philadelphians and an extra round of entertaining stimulated.

John Adams, who loved his stomach, literally drooled over a dinner he partook of at the Hills, the home of Robert Morris.

The gentlemen of the Schuylkill Hills were all Loyalists at first and Robert Morris, as a Pennsylvania delegate to Congress steadily voted against an open rupture with England. The men stayed late at the coffee houses and taverns in earnest discussions, arriving at their country seats in the small hours of dawn. Besides Morris as a delegate, his neighbor Charles Thomson was the Secretary of the Congress.

Matters grew from bad to worse and finally Paul Revere arrived with the news of the Battle of Lexington. Fully realizing what they were doing and the serious consequences of their actions some of the Hillers like Morris, Thomson, and Macpherson became active Patriots, while others like Galloway, Franks, and Samuel Shoemaker remained loyal to the British crown. Their various careers are told in connection with the story of their estates.

When the actual fighting was over and the bitterness against the Tories subsided, many families returned to the Hills and the

6

old routine of life was somewhat resumed, stimulated by the presence of President Washington and the Diplomatic Corps, as Philadelphia was now the capital of the budding nation.

Time passed, a younger generation took over and more mansions were built, roads were improved, even the water way became more accessible. Life continued gracious and hospitable although with a more modern touch and minus the powdered wigs and pompadours, until the building of the dam which forced the exodus from a now unhealthy spot.

FAIRMOUNT WATER WORKS, AQUARIUM

IN THE beginning the water for the City of Philadelphia was supplied by individual wells and public pumps. Then in 1801 a water works was housed in Center Square, in a building designed by Benjamin Henry Latrobe, which was considered the first extensive water system since the times of the Romans. But Philadelphia was growing and Latrobe's waterworks rapidly became inadequate, so in 1812 the City purchased five acres of land on the east bank of the Schuylkill River including Faire Mount, which was to be the reservoir.

At first a series of steam pumps raised the water to the reservoir, but when the dam was built in 1822 the water power derived from this was used. The engineer for the new waterworks was Frederick Graff who had been associated with Latrobe. The area

7

was carefully landscaped and some statues placed in appropriate spots. To protect the water supply the City purchased some more property extending through Lemon Hill. Practically from the beginning the place became so popular that Councils decided to create a public park and to add to the holdings from time to time, so that by 1828 the five acres had grown to twenty-four. These were the beginnings of Fairmount Park. The small classical temples at either end of the waterworks served as a meeting place for the "watering committee" and a place for the caretaker. The central Grecian part, known as the Graff Mansion, was the Ball Room, site of many receptions for foreign dignitaries and other important visitors who, after being greeted, were taken to inspect the building and machinery which had made architectural and engineering history. The waterworks were decked over to form a promenade for spectators to enjoy the beauty of the water falling over the dam and the general charming landscaping surrounding the building.

Two little classic temples were added in strategic spots, supposedly inspired by Le Notre's Temple d'Amour at Chantilly in France. Even today this area is a gem of the park. Taverns were opened like Rialto's and Harding's Hotel to cater to the increasing populace.

By the early 20th Century the Fairmount reservoir ceased to be the source of the City water supply and in 1911 the machinery was sold and the building became a public Aquarium and Museum of Aquatic Life. The State Legislature provided the tanks and the Pennsylvania State Fish and Game and the Forestry Protective Association supplied the finances and the fish. The Aquarium was opened to the public on Thanksgiving Day, November 24, 1911. It came under the jurisdiction of the Park Commission the following year. In 1921 the title was changed to Fairmount Park Aquarium.

In December, 1962, all the fish and tanks were finally removed and the premises are now occupied by the Street Tree office of the Park Commission and the J. B. Kelly Foundation for Swimming Pool Training. Faire Mount is now the site of the Philadelphia Museum of Art.[2]

2-See page 83

THE ESTATES

EAST BANK

THE HILLS, LEMON HILL

THE SITE of the Hills was originally part of William Penn's Springettsbury Manor.

Penn started a vineyard there and folklore states that he placed a gardener in a small house thereon, familiar with grape culture. The place at that time was locally called "Old Vinegar." Robert Morris purchased it from Tench Francis and built a house on the Hills in 1770.

Morris was a big man, over six feet tall, and did everything in a big way. He was a partner in the mercantile house of Willing and Morris, the largest importing and exporting firm in the Colonies, and was greatly respected and admired by his contemporaries. He was a "master of satire which was as artistic as it was pointed and confounding and had a diverting wit which he brought to bear upon every discussion." Morris married Molly White, the sister of William White, the first Episcopal Bishop of Pennsylvania, and they had several children.

Mrs. Morris was an able, cultured, gracious lady, thoroughly capable of directing her vast household and constant lavish entertainments.

As a merchant in the European, West Indian, and China trade, Morris imported freely for his own household "many items that were too choice for the American trade."

Their life on the Hills was similar to their neighbors, but on a far more extravagant scale.

Morris had a town house and used the Hills as a Country Summer seat. The property consisted of 140 acres and 97 perches. He subsequently added to this property so that he eventually possessed about 300 acres. Morris recorded that the Hills contained "two farm houses with barns, stables, cow houses, springhouses . . . a large garden with the best fruit trees . . . a large green house with two hot houses as proper fireplaces. These and everything necessary . . . by far the compleatest of anything of the kind in America."

Like his neighbors, Morris was strongly adverse to a final break with England and did his best to prevent it as a delegate to the Continental Congress, but when the die was cast at Lexington he sided wholeheartedly with the Patriots. When the Revolution broke out and Howe threatened Philadelphia, Mrs. Morris and the children went to Maryland to stay with her step sister while Morris remained to run the Government in the absence of Congress. Morris wrote to his wife, "I have been constantly prepared, my things packed up, horses and carriages ready at any moment. I dine at the Hills today and have done so every Sunday. Thus you see, I continue my old practice of mixing business with pleasure; I have ever found them useful to each other."

The threat passed for the moment and Mrs. Morris returned, but Howe's advance became a reality in 1777 so the Morris family departed for Manheim "taking all that they valued most of their household effects, travelling in a caravan of Conestoga wagons, to occupy Baron Stiegel's Big House," where Mrs. Morris continued her hospitable way of life for the numerous emissaries travelling back and forth.

Meanwhile, Morris and John Hancock were running the Colonial Government. Morris was organizing the infant Navy for defense, directing the fleeing populace with their goods and chattels, and on his own credit raising fifty thousand badly needed dollars to pay the troops.

When the Morrises moved out of the Hills, the British soldiers moved in and stationed an outpost there.

When the Morrises returned on the departure of the British. they found the whole place a shambles.

Robert Morris slowly restored the Hills and in the meantime rented Lansdowne as a summer resort. When Washington visited Morris in 1795 they dined in the green house at the Hills.

Gradually Philadelphia regained its prestige and life became nearly normal once more. More Congresses were held and General Washington came to stay at the Hills. Morris was instrumental in having Philadelphia declared the Capital while Washington, D. C. was in the making.

With the advent of the President and his Cabinet, the round of entertainments struck a new high, augmented by the Diplomatic Corps and their entourage. The intimacy formed in the early Congressional days between the Washingtons and the Morrises became even closer. Mrs. Morris was always at Mrs. Washington's right hand and was considered the Second Lady of the land. Morris, as head of the Office of Finance, performed herculean tasks in keeping the empty government coffers replenished. His daring activities in this connction during the most critical moments of the Revolution make a book in themselves, and Washington never forgot it.

During Washington's and part of Adams' administrations the Hills was the scene of happy times again, but tragedy was approaching.

Ever optimistic and with a firm belief in the future of the United States, Morris invested heavily in real estate. As usual, he did it in a big way, buying up enormous tracts and whole blocks of the future city of Washington. Unfortunately, he was before his time and even his great credit could not carry his investments. Creditors arose in every direction and Morris was forced to hide at the Hills to avoid being arrested and sent to the debtors' prison. His failure, like everything he did, was colossal. With his affluent background and surroundings what mental agonies he must have endured as he saw all his investments stripped away at a great loss, and himself and family reduced to poverty. Protected by his faithful gardener, James, and his dogs, he remained at the Hills until matters became hopeless and he gave himself up. After languishing in the debtors' prison for three years, he died a broken man at his son's house in Morrisville, the village named after him, in 1806.

A bitter ending for the man who had financed the Revolution!

The Hills was sold at sheriff's sale. Henry Pratt, another rich merchant, purchased part of the estate in 1799. Like his predecessor, he invested in real estate, but more conservatively. At one time he owned the land which Wanamakers and Caldwells now occupy.

In the U. S. District Tax Records the part that Pratt purchased contained two houses. It is not stated what they were, but we know the greenhouse survived because among the exotic plants that were still there were the lemon trees which gave Pratt the idea of calling the place "Lemon Hill."

Henry Pratt was the son of Matthew Pratt, an artist and pupil of Benjamin West. Henry was reputed to be of a strong character and persevering. He married three times and had fifteen children, but outlived them all, dying in 1838.

Besides his marital activities, Pratt took a prominent part in civic affairs. He was President of the Delaware Fire Company, member of the Chamber of Commerce, Vestryman of Christ Church, and President of Select Council. In 1738 he was made Riding Pay Master for all stages between Philadelphia and Newport, Virginia. When the War of 1812 broke out, Pratt was the second member to be appointed by the General Committee of Superintendence for the Protection of the River Delaware and the City of Philadelphia. Henry Pratt spent a fortune on Lemon Hill, building the present house and embellishing the grounds with ponds, fountains, statuary and summer houses. Here he entertained in as lavish a style as Robert Morris.

On Pratt's death the property was sold at sheriff's sale to the Bank of the United States, which failed and the City of Philadelphia acquired it. City Council pondered as to whether to turn the property into a cemetery or sell it off for development. The estate was saved for posterity by 27 petitions signed by 2,443 civic minded citizens in 1844 to have it made into a public park. In 1855 forty-five acres, including the mansion, were officially proclaimed Fairmount Park. For some years the house and immediate grounds were leased as a beer garden mostly frequented by the German population of the city who held frequent singing festivities there.

When Fiske Kimball became Director of the then building Philadelphia Museum of Art in 1925, he was given the pretty dilapidated neighboring house at Lemon Hill in which to live. Kimball and his wife, Marie Goebel Kimball, with the assistance of the Fairmount Park Commission, restored and furnished the handsome mansion in 18th Century style.

Both Kimballs died in 1955 and for a short interval Lemon Hill was empty. It is now occupied by the Colonial Dames of America, Chapter II.[3]

SEDGLEY

THIS at one time was part of the Hills Estate. It was sold to William Cramond in 1799 who called it Sedgley, and built a house on it that year, designed by Benjamin Latrobe and considered the "earliest Gothic country residence in America." Cramond failed in 1806 and Samuel Mifflin added the property to his real estate investments. From about 1812 to 1836 James Cowles Fisher rented it as a summer home. In 1836 Isaac S. Loyd purchased it and tried to make a development of the property, but was unsuccessful. The City bought the place in 1857. By that time the house was in such ill repair it was demolished and the Gate House turned into the present Sedgley Park Guard House.

3-See page 83

ORMISTON

A HOUSE was built on this property by Joseph Galloway sometime before the Revolution.

Joseph Galloway was born in West River, Anne Arundel County, Maryland, about 1730, one of the Galloways of Tulip Hill.

He came to Philadelphia as a young man and became a successful lawyer. He married Grace, a daughter of Lawrence Growdon, a leading Quaker, and through her inherited an estate in Bucks County which was to become his refuge in times of trouble.

Galloway entered the Assembly in 1757 and became the Speaker from 1765 to 1777.

Owing to his outspoken loyalty to the British Crown, he refused to sit in the Second Congress. Galloway joined the British forces in 1776 and was Provost Marshal of Philadelphia during their occupation of the city.

Ormiston was promptly confiscated and Galloway fled to his place in Bucks County until he departed for England with Lord Howe, and died there in 1803.

He had called his "good house on Schuylkill, Ormiston after ye name of our Grandfather's Seat near Edinburgh."

Princeton University bestowed an LL.D. on him in 1769 and among his civic activities he drew the plans for the old Germantown Academy in 1759.

James Hutchinson, M.D., purchased the tract and house in 1781. Actual money was so scarce in the Colonies, the General Assembly passed an Act, November 27, 1779, providing "that one-fourth of the purchase money should remain in the hands of the purchaser paying interest for same to be reduced into species at the rate of $60 of the then bills of credit of the United States for one Spanish milled dollar to be charged on the premises as a yearly rent to be payable in good merchantable wheat at 10 shillings per bushel." To add to the complications the Trustees of the University of Pennsylvania also collected a yearly ground rent of 12-2/10 bushels of wheat. This ground rent was redeemable for 1,183 bushels of wheat.

General Joseph Reed purchased Ormiston in 1781. Reed was a lawyer who had studied at the Middle Temple in London. He joined Washington's Army and at the Battle of Whitemarsh had his horse shot from under him.

In 1778 he became president of the Supreme Executive Council of Pennsylvania.

General Reed lived at Ormiston until he died, when his executors sold the property to Edward Burd, 1798.

Burd's first action was to extinguish the ground rent of the University of Pennsylvania. He is credited with adding the front porch, 1798.

The City purchased the property in 1869.

The upper story is occupied by a Park Guard and for a while the Fairmount Park Art Association had an office downstairs.[4] The rest of the first floor is used by Day Camps for handicapped children under the auspices of the Philadelphia Department of Recreation.

RANDOLPH MANSION, LAUREL HILL

ALTHOUGH this was also called Laurel Hill it is not to be confused with Laurel Hill Cemetery which is on quite a different property.

Laurel Hill is next to Ormiston and received its name from the luxuriant thickets of native laurel which once covered the bluffs above the river.

The house is of Georgian architecture and was erected by Joseph Shute about 1748.

Shute lived quietly and did not partake of his neighbors' gay lives.

When the place was purchased by Francis Rawle in 1760, the scene changed considerably.

Francis Rawle was an only child and inherited a considerable fortune. As a young man he made "the grand tour of Europe" and became a cultured gentleman of many interests. In 1756 he had married Rebecca Warner, daughter of Edward Warner, a

4-See page 83

wealthy and prominent citizen. Francis Rawle did not enjoy Laurel Hill long, for he was accidentally killed while shooting near the Delaware in 1761.

Mrs. Rawle, with her three small children, continued to occupy Laurel Hill during the summer months and in 1767 married Samuel Shoemaker. Shoemaker was a widower also with several children. From then on they divided their time between Laurel Hill and the Shoemaker place in Germantown.

Shoemaker was also a courtly gentleman with considerable means of his own.

Under the Royal and Proprietary governments he held many important posts including Mayor of Philadelphia, City Treasurer, member of the Provincial Assembly and Judge in the County Courts. Until the Revolution the Shoemakers had much in common with their neighbors on the Hills and there was the usual visiting back and forth.

When the Revolution broke out the combined Shoemaker family remained loyal to England and were forced to flee to New York when the British departed from Philadelphia. During the British occupation of the city, Shoemaker assisted Joseph Galloway in administering the civil affairs. When Shoemaker went to London with the departing British, young William Rawle accompanied him.

Laurel Hill was confiscated and Mrs. Shoemaker, who had tarried, was ordered to leave Philadelphia and not return without leave of Council. This intrepid woman calmly ignored the order and lived quietly at Laurel Hill for a year, only departing to see her husband and son off to England.

In 1782 Shoemaker's life interest in his wife's estate, which included Laurel Hill, was sold to Major James Parr, an extensive investor in confiscated properties.

Parr leased Laurel Hill to the French Minister Chevalier de la Luzerne.

The Chevalier was a good musician and so was his secretary, Captain Louis Otto, and there were many musicales at the mansion during the summer.

When the War was over and the bitterness against the Loyalists had somewhat subsided; with considerable difficulty Mrs. Shoemaker was able to gain possession of Laurel Hill, where she lived until her death.

In 1828 William Rawle sold Laurel Hill to Dr. Philip Syng Physick who purchased it as a wedding present for his daughter, Mrs. Jacob Randolph. From then on the property was known as the Randolph Mansion.

Jacob Randolph was a prominent Philadelphian. He was one of the surgeons connected with the Pennsylvania Hospital and Professor of Clinical Surgery of the University of Pennsylvania.

The Randolph family occupied Laurel Hill until 1869 when it was sold to the city.

STRAWBERRY MANSION, SOMERTON

THERE WAS a farm house standing on the site of Strawberry Mansion, possibly as early as 1768, belonging to the Hood family who owned down to the river. A ford across the river from their property to the Roberts tract, Pencoyd, on the west bank was called the Robin Hood ford and gave the idea to the Park Commission to call the outdoor concert stadium, situated in the dell below Strawberry Mansion, the name of Robin Hood Dell.

Charles Thomson and his wife, Hannah Norris Harrison

Thomson, altered the house to suit their convenience and lived there from 1774 to 1777. The place was then called Somerton. Charles Thomson came to America at the age of 10. His widower father died during the crossing leaving Charles and his younger brother to the care of the Captain. On landing, the Captain apprenticed Charles to a blacksmith in New Castle. The little fellow was a studious, intelligent boy far above the level of his blacksmith employer, so he promptly ran away and came to Philadelphia. Grown a man he became a teacher of languages at the Franklin Academy and took a prominent part in civic affairs. The Indians respected him so much that the powerful Tedyuscung refused to hold parley with the white men unless Thomson was present.

When the first Continental Congress was assembled, Thomson was made secretary. When the British came to Philadelphia, Lord Howe hoped to find incriminating papers at Somerton and sent his soldiers to investigate. Mrs. Thomson was warned by friendly Indians and fled across the river to her ancestral home, Harriton.

Frustrated, the soldiers burnt Somerton, 1777.

The ruins stood neglected until Judge William Lewis purchased the property, 1797-98.

Lewis constructed what he called "a simple country summer home" and while it was being built rented the nearby Woodford.

Judge Lewis was a prominent Quaker and with the assistance of Drs. Rush and Franklin drew up the first law against slavery ever passed by any government in the world.

Lewis was quite an individualist, over six feet tall, with a deep baritone voice, which was used to effect in trying a case. "When he was not arguing a case, he was quizzing or joking or mooting or smoking, generally in a state of unrest. . . ." "Destitute of almost all dimensions but length," he was "immensely proud of the attitude and length of his nose." Another friend said his "distinguished ugliness" made him engaging and "when he took off his spectacles the expression of his eyes was kindly."

President Washington and Alexander Hamilton frequently rode out to Somerton, where they retired to the point overlooking the river for privacy and discussed the constitutional interpretation of banking laws with Judge Lewis.

The first Mrs. Lewis, mother of the Lewis children, died at Somerton and shortly afterwards Lewis married a well-born Irish widow named Frances Durdin. Lewis liked to read plays and act them as he read and Frances loved music. She persuaded the Judge to buy her a piano—a shocking action to most of their Quaker friends. Frances and William both sang and the walls of Somerton were gay once more.

On the death of Judge Lewis, 1819, Mrs. Lewis returned to Ireland and another Quaker Judge from Chester County purchased Somerton, after it had been rented to various people.

Judge Joseph Hemphill had married Margaret Coleman, daughter of a wealthy iron baron, and they had two sons, Alexander and Coleman. Alexander died young and from then on nothing was too good for Coleman.

The Hemphills were active and fond of entertaining. They added fountains and a formal garden and, to please Coleman, a race track. Mrs. Hemphill was an excellent horsewoman and often rode with Coleman. While the Judge was busy in the city with business and civic affairs, young Coleman grew up to be a country squire. He imported strawberries from Chile which were supposed to have an excellent flavor, but more likely the frequent application of fertilizer from the cow barn deserves the credit. The Hemphills prided themselves on their herd.

In 1827 when the senior Hemphills returned from one of their trips to Europe they were greeted with a new wing on the house added by Coleman for a ball room, so the Judge constructed another wing on the opposite side to gain an architectural balance.

In 1831 Judge Hemphill became a partner of William Ellis Tucker in his newly established china factory. Tucker was the first successful manufacturer of porcelain in America.

The bank failure of 1833 ruined Hemphill and he was forced to sell his share in the factory and mortgage Somerton.

At the Judge's death Somerton was sold to a Mrs. George Cook, who ultimately sold it to the Steward of the Philadelphia Club who opened a restaurant in the mansion, specializing in the famous strawberries and rich cream from the remaining cows, 1846.

At this time there was a small excursion steamer running on the Schuylkill which stopped at the old landings and passengers got to asking to be left off at the Strawberry landing. Gradually the mansion and finally the whole area went by that name. Many of the boat clubs entertained at Strawberry. Strawberry Mansion became Park property in 1867 and in 1876 the mansion and grounds became a beer garden with a bandstand. In 1890 it changed its nationality and was an Italian resort with dance music, red wine and the aroma of garlic.

In 1900 another change took place—sailors on leave had a rendezvous with cooperating ladies on the second floor, a police court and recreation area for the park guards used the first floor, while rumor had it that a speak-easy operated in the cellar. Finally the sailors and police and possible bartenders were evacuated and the Committee of 1926 took over in 1929.

The Committee of 1926 was composed of members of the Women's Committee for the Sesqui-Centennial Exposition in Philadelphia. The mansion was a shambles and the grounds partly occupied as a playground. The Park Commission removed the playground equipment and the ladies restored and refurnished the mansion so successfully that within a year it was opened to the public as their headquarters and "House of Hospitality where members can give parties."[5]

Strawberry Mansion is the only house in the park furnished in the Empire style.

5-See page 84

H.T. MACNEILL '64

WOODFORD

THERE WAS an existing farm house on the site which was remodeled by William Coleman in 1756. It was again added to in 1772. The original stable is still standing.

The one story farm house had been built near what was known as the Wissahickon road, the main artery out of Philadelphia along the Schuylkill to Norristown via the mouth of the Wissahickon Creek.

Tradition has it that the forest of trees which had to be cleared and the nearby ford across the river gave the place its name.

William Coleman held many important offices in Provincial Pennsylvania and was a man of wide experience and cultured tastes. Franklin said of him that he "had the coolest, clearest head, the best heart, and the exactest morals of almost any man I ever met with." In fact Franklin had such a respect for him, he stated in his will that his wife, Deborah, and son William should go to Coleman for advice and council.

Coleman was a founder of the Junto, treasurer of the Philadelphia Library Company, trustee of the Academy, later the University of Pennsylvania, at various times a Justice of the Peace, member of City Council, County Court Judge and a justice of the Provincial Pennsylvania Supreme Court.

Although Coleman was married, he did not have any children and when he died he left Woodford to his nephew. The house proved too small for the nephew and his eight children so it was sold to Alexander Barclay.

Barclay was His Majesty's Comptroller of Customs and only used Woodford as a summer residence. He died two years later without making any alterations, but his short tenure established Woodford as a prominent Tory sphere.

After Barclay's death in 1771, the house came into the possession of Mrs. Barclay's sister and her husband, Mr. and Mrs. David Franks.

David Franks was a Jewish aristocrat and belonged to the Philadelphia Dancing Assemblies. Besides being a successful merchant, he was the Crown agent for Philadelphia.

The Franks had four children so they enlarged the house. The Franks were a most welcome addition to the Hill colony, and there was much inter-visiting.

When the Revolution broke out the Franks remained Loyalists and made a point of entertaining Lord Howe and his officers.

The daughter Rebecca was a charmer and a flirt and Woodford became a happy break in the boredom of living in Philadelphia, especially for the young officers who were stationed in unwilling households. Tradition has it that Lord Howe rode out to Woodford daily, while the officers composed poems satirizing the leading patriots, to entertain the fair Rebecca. At the famous Mischianza Ball, given as a farewell to Lord Howe in 1778, the lovely Rebecca was chosen to lead the dancing.

When the British departed Woodford became almost a house of mourning.

Although David Franks had signed the Non-Importation Agreement against the Stamp Act and later, at the request of the Continental Congress, was appointed to provide for the British prisoners, the doings at Woodford had been too prominent to escape notice. Late in 1778 a letter Franks wrote to his brother in London was intercepted and gave the Patriots the excuse they had been looking for. Benedict Arnold, now military governor of Philadelphia, was directed to arrest him on the charge of giving information to the enemy.

Franks still had powerful friends and he was acquitted. In

spite of the warning Franks tried to smuggle another letter to Major André in New York. This was really playing with fire. Again he was arrested, but got off with the light sentence of being ordered to leave the country. Accordingly, the Franks family departed in 1780 for New York to be under the protection of Clinton. Woodford was confiscated and sold to Thomas Paschall and it was later rented to Judge William Lewis while the latter was rebuilding Somerton. It was while the judge was at Woodford that Washington and Hamilton rode out from town to consult him. They would leave their horses at Woodford and then the three gentlemen walked out to a seat on the bluff at Somerton overlooking the river, where they could have privacy for their discussions.

Isaac Wharton was the next owner of Woodford. Wharton had grown up at his father's place, Walnut Grove, the scene of the Mischianza Ball, and there must have been times, when he wandered through the halls of Woodford, that the spirit of the gay Rebecca and her triumphal career could have visited him.

During the Wharton regime the additions to Woodford were completed and the mansion remained in the family until after the Civil War.

The dread "river fever" probably drove them away, but the place was cared for and not allowed to deteriorate.

Woodford became a part of Fairmount Park in 1868 and for a while in 1912 was used as a Park Guard Headquarters. The handsome mantel was boarded over and the drawing room converted into a court in which to try offenders against Park rules. These culprits were mostly hot rod nouveau motorists, who were apprehended by the Park bicycle squad! The saying was that the Guards' mustaches were as wide as the handle bars on the bicycles.

Miss Naomi Wood, a noted Philadelphia collector of everything pertaining to American life, from handsome furniture to household equipment, died in 1926 leaving her possessions in perpetual trust for display as "an illustration of household gear during Colonial years" and made a fellow collector, Mr. Daniel Huntoon, her trustee. Seeking a suitable place in which to exhibit this collection, Mr. Huntoon approached the Park Commission for a house in the Park.

Woodford was selected and from 1928-30 the mansion was carefully renovated by the architect, John P. B. Sinkler, who had been a former City Architect of Philadelphia and, with the collaboration of the Philadelphia Museum of Art, it was opened to the public early in 1930.

Mr. Huntoon's own collection was subsequently added and arranged so successfully that a visitor receives the impression that the family is still in residence.

Woodford is open to the public.[6]

ROCKLAND

THE ORIGINAL Patent from William Penn to Mary Rotchford, widow of Dennis Rotchford, for this site is dated 1693-4.

Mrs. Rotchford sold the property to Thomas Shute in that same year. He seems to have just held it for an investment, or maybe farmed it.

In 1754, Abel James had some dealings with Joseph Shute, son of Thomas, purchasing part of the property, with the rest going to a John Lawrence. The deed describes Lawrence's tract as "Beginning at a White Oak Stump on the Banks of the River Schuylkill and from thence running along the lines of Joseph

Galloway (of Ormiston) . . . to a Road laid out by the same Joseph Shute for the accommodation of the purchasers."

The property went through several hands until 1809 when it was purchased by George Thompson, who built the house in 1810, at which time it was considered one of the handsomest Federal architectural dwellings in Philadelphia. It contains a graceful curved stairs of two flights, plaster ceilings and groove-and-rosette woodwork, typical of the late Federal era.

The property was added to the Park in 1869.[7]

HATFIELD HOUSE, THE PLACE

THE HOUSE was built in 1760 and originally stood at the corner of Hunting Park and Pulaski Avenues. In 1835 the house was modernized and sheathed with flush board siding, an unusual addition in the Philadelphia area. Originally a simple farm house of two stories, Dr. Nathan Lewis Hatfield purchased it and transformed it into a gentleman's country seat, using it as his summer home.

Dr. Hatfield was a member of the first class graduated from the Jefferson Medical College in 1826 and practiced for over sixty years. His son, Major Henry Reed Hatfield, had his ancestral home pulled down piece by piece and re-erected in Fairmount Park in 1930 at his own expense, at the same time underwriting a

7-See page 84

perpetual fire insurance policy on it, and presented the mansion, furnished, to the City.

Major Hatfield was a member of the First Troop Philadelphia City Cavalry, an officer of the National Guard, member of the St. Anthony Club, and president of the Yorktown Historical Society of the United States, the members of which organizations were all entertained at The Place, from time to time.

In 1960 the mansion was refurbished by the Pennsylvania Chapter of the National Society of Interior Designers.

Among other historical papers and scientific books, the house contains letters written by Colonel Tench Tilghman.

MOUNT PLEASANT, CLUNIE

MOUNT PLEASANT was built by Captain John Macpherson in 1761.

Captain Macpherson came from an old Scottish Highland family. He was an active, crusty sort of man, but he had a kindly side too.

The Captain made his money in privateering, in the course of which he was wounded several times. John Adams wrote that Macpherson had had his arm "shot off twice"!

Macpherson was married twice, having several children by his first wife. The second was also Scottish and that prolific writer, John Adams, reported that she was clever and the daughters pretty. There were two sons, John, Jr., who went to Princeton and became a promising young lawyer; while the Captain purchased a commission in the British Army for the other son, William.

Besides his mercantile interests, the Captain was something of an inventor. Among other things he constructed a bug-proof bed. He called it an "elegant cot which bids defiance to everything but omnipotence."

Until John and William went away to school and the Army, the Macphersons all dwelt happily at Mount Pleasant and the house resounded to the merry shouts of children, while as social leaders, the adults gave many parties.

Macpherson had first called his mansion "Clunie" after his native home in Scotland, when he purchased the property from Benjamin Mifflin, but they were all so happy on their hill, Mount Pleasant seemed more appropriate. Macpherson built his house at the height of the Chippendale fashion in America when Philadelphia was the artistic center of the Colonies and Mount Pleasant is an outstanding example of handsome Georgian architecture both inside and out. Macpherson sided enthusiastically with the Patriots during the Revolution and his son John volunteered and went as Aide-de-Camp to General Montgomery on his expedition to Canada, while the British refused to accept William's resignation from the Army.

The Captain spent most of his time in the city busy with helping to organize the infant Patriot Navy while the little household at Mount Pleasant occupied themselves with war activities, sewing for the soldiers, etc., trying to forget the heartache waiting for news of the boys.

The first blow fell when a travel stained rider and weary horse arrived at Mount Pleasant with the tragic tidings that young John Macpherson had been killed at the side of his General in the assault on Quebec. Captain Macpherson had had such high hopes for him. One can picture that sad family and the broken-hearted Captain with bowed head slowly limping up the great staircase to his room where he shut the door to be alone with his grief.

William, forced to remain in the British Army, was present at the Battle of Monmouth, where he was ironically wounded while standing idly by.

When Dr. Benjamin Rush was sent by Washington to treat the wounded Americans after the battle, he mentions in his diary that William was one of his patients.

William's resignation was finally accepted by Sir Henry Clinton, with the proviso that he could not leave New York. William made a most dramatic escape and joined the American Army with a rank of Major. William had a most active subsequent career. In 1789 he was made Surveyor of the Port of Philadelphia, in 1792 he became Inspector of Revenue for the city, and in 1793 he became a Naval officer. In 1794, Governor Mifflin commissioned him Colonel in command of a battalion of state troops known as the Macpherson Blues and in 1799 President Adams commissioned him Brigadier General of the Provisional Army raised to suppress Fries' Rebellion.

General Macpherson was one of the original members of the Society of the Cincinnati. His civic activities included serving as a delegate to the Pennsylvania Convention to ratify the Constitution, member of the Pennsylvania Assembly and president of the St. Andrew's Society.

To return to the Captain. Not wishing to dwell longer in a house with such sad memories, Macpherson rented Mount Pleasant to the Spanish Minister, Don Juan de Mirailles, and it became the scene of many colorful diplomatic receptions.

In town the Captain busied himself with publishing the "Price Currant" every two weeks, quoting the latest foreign prices, which could be consulted by anyone who would "put six pence or more into the charity box for the relief of widows and orphans dependent upon the sea-captains' club" and inventing gadgets such as a contraption for moving houses and the aforementioned bug-proof bed. In between these occupations, he gave lectures on astronomy and in 1785 published the first city directory.

In 1779 Benedict Arnold, who was acting military governor

of Philadelphia, purchased Mount Pleasant as a gift for his bride, Peggy Shippen, but they never lived there.

Blair McClenachan was the next prominent owner. McClenachan had also made a fortune in privateering. He was a high tempered Irishman and helped Robert Morris finance the Revolution. Truly Irish he sympathized with the French Revolution and was a strong Jeffersonian. He sat in the Pennsylvania legislature from 1790 to 1795 and in Congress from 1797 to 1799.

In 1792 Judge Jonathan Williams, a great-nephew of Benjaman Franklin, purchased Mount Pleasant.

Williams was born in Boston in 1750 and went to London with his brother in 1770 to complete their mercantile training under the guidance of great Uncle Ben.

In 1796 he was appointed Associate Judge in the Court of Common Pleas.

Through his activities in the American Philosophical Society he met Jefferson who, in 1801, made him inspector of fortifications and superintendent at West Point with the rank of major. He was the first superintendent of the Military Academy. During the War of 1812 he was brevetted Brigadier-General of the New York militia and was on the committee in Philadelphia to fortify the Delaware River.

Although General Williams died in 1815, Mount Pleasant remained in the family until annexed by the Park in 1868.

While living in Mount Pleasant Williams carried on many experiments assisted by great Uncle Ben. The spirit of the Old Captain probably took a keen interest too.

For a short time during the early days of automobiles when lady drivers were the exception, the mansion was the headquarters of a club of feminine drivers called the Movaganto Klubo. It was organized by Miss Madge Corlies who was instrumental in starting the Sedgely Club. In 1925 through the generosity of Charles H. Ludington the mansion was restored and furnished by the Philadelphia Museum of Art. It is considered one of the finest houses in the Park and is open to the public daily.[8]

8-See page 84

ARNEST

THERE ARE very few records available about this small property.

The house is thought to have been built between 1800 and 1810 and takes its name from the last owner. It is of English Regency architecture and contains some fine woodwork and a rare pseudo-bamboo molding with lotus flower brackets in the stair and a handsome reeded mantel in the north bedroom.

It is not open to the public.

THE CLIFFS

THIS PROPERTY was purchased from the Mifflin family in 1753 by Joshua Fisher, and the place remained in the Fisher family until acquired by the Park Commission in 1869.

Joshua built the house in 1757 and it is wainscoted throughout.

During the Revolution, Samuel R. Fisher, a direct descendant of Joshua, remained loyal to the British Crown and was forced to flee from the Cliffs into the back country.

Sarah Franklin Bache, daughter of Benjamin Franklin, rented the house and made it a headquarters for a ladies' sewing circle to make clothing and bandages for the Patriot soldiers.

In 1934 Erling H. Pederson, then the official architect for the Philadelphia Museum of Art, occupied the dwelling.

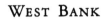

WEST BANK

THE SOLITUDE

THIS TRACT of land was not in the original Penn grant, but was purchased by John Penn, grandson of William Penn, who erected the house in 1785. He is supposed to have called the place The Solitude after the Duke of Wurtenburg's house of similar name, but as John was a poet and also had a house in town it is more likely that he meant it for a retreat in which to study and compose.

John was the son of Thomas Penn and Lady Juliana Fermor, daughter of the Earl of Pomfret.

He was a cultured, scholarly man with a Master of Arts degree from Cambridge University. Before coming to America he had traveled extensively. He was a patron of the arts as well as a poet and an idealist. John designed Solitude based on the Brothers Adam style of architecture and it was the first of its kind in America and shortly to be followed by many others. The house is a gem with a beautiful wrought iron stairrail and handsome Sheraton bookcases still in place. There are Adamesque plaster ceilings in the library and parlor. Besides a bowling green and flower garden, he kept a herd of deer controlled by a ha-ha, a type of English sunken barrier, and the forerunner of the Zoological Garden which presently surrounds the mansion.

Life at Solitude was not all studious. Penn gave gay parties, the guests coming by boat from Philadelphia; and Washington is known to have spent a day there while attending the Constitutional Convention in Philadelphia.

John Penn returned to England in 1788 where he led a prominent and active life. On his death he left Solitude to his brother, Granville Penn.

For a short time Governor Richard Penn occupied the house. Then for forty years it remained in the care of a caretaker. In 1851 Granville John Penn visited it. Granville was much lionized by the Philadelphians and he gave a "Fête Champêtre" at Solitude with marquees and a grand collation "to which the quality of the city was invited."

This was the last time a Penn was at Solitude, a fitting if not a Quaker farewell.

Solitude returned to the caretaker until 1869 when the Park Commission acquired it.

For a short time after the Penns sold the land the West Philadelphia Waterworks was situated on part of the property.[9]

9-See page 84

LETITIA STREET HOUSE, WILLIAM PENN HOUSE

THOMAS CHALKLEY, a Philadelphia merchant, bought the lot on Letitia Street, a small alley or court paralleling Market Street from Front to Second Street, for an investment in 1707. The alley or court was named after William Penn's daughter, Letitia. John Smart, a house carpenter, built the house between 1713 and 1715. He never lived there and it was probably rented. Joshua Gee, a London merchant, purchased the property from Chalkley in 1722 and may have used it as a base for his American contacts. On his death in 1730 his sons Samuel and Osgood Gee inherited it and sold it to Oswald Peel in 1735. Peel was a mariner merchant and actually lived in the house until he built a more handsome mansion called "Greenhedge" on the site of Girard College.

Peel died in 1765 and his daughter, Mrs. Francis Hariss, became the possessor.

In 1883 the house was purchased by the City and removed to Fairmount Park, where through the generosity of Mr. and Mrs. Henry Paul Busch it was restored and furnished in the Queen Anne Style in 1932, and opened to the public.

When the Schuylkill Expressway was built access to the house was cut off, so the furniture which had been on loan from the Art Museum was removed and the windows boarded up.

In the spring of 1967 it was decided to refurbish the house under the auspices of the Art Museum and construct a driveway. The house should be open to the public in the near future.

Letitia Street House is a rare example of Eighteenth Century row-house architecture and quite individual among the Park houses.

CEDAR GROVE

CEDAR GROVE originally stood in Harrowgate near Frankford and was the home of five generations of Paschalls and Morrises. The land belonged to George Habell who had quite an investment in what was then a popular residential environ of Philadelphia. He was a weaver. Elizabeth Coats Paschall, wife of Joseph Paschall, built a simple farm house on the property for a summer residence for herself and her three children.[10] By 1748 the family had grown and Mrs. Paschall added to the house. Mrs. Paschall died in 1768 and Beulah Paschall inherited the home. The next owner was her niece, Sarah, who married Isaac Wistar Morris in 1795. Morris was no relation to Robert Morris of the Hills, but a grandson of Caspar Wistar, the well-known glass manufacturer of New Jersey. The Isaac Morrises again added to Cedar Grove, Morris being his own architect.

Their eldest son, Isaac Paschall Morris, next came into possession in 1831 and finally John and Lydia Morris of Compton, Chestnut Hill, became the final owners. By 1888 the surroundings had become so industrialized it was no longer pleasant to summer

10-See page 84

at Cedar Grove so Mr. and Miss Morris closed up the house and moved all the furnishings to Compton. After brother John's death, Miss Lydia had the house taken apart stone by stone and re-erected in Fairmount Park as a gift to the City in 1927. Some of the old panes of glass have names and dates on them.

She replaced all the furnishings so that today it stands in simple Quaker dignity with its furnishings reflecting the taste and life of the Quaker family that owned it.

There is a tradition that a gentle ghost inhabits the house, a young Quaker lady, who is occasionally seen beckoning a welcome from a second story window.

The Herb Society of Philadelphia has planted a charming garden at the side of the house.

Cedar Grove is open to the public.[11]

Sweet Briar, Fairmount Park 1797

SWEETBRIER, PETERSTONE

SWEETBRIER was built by Samuel Breck in 1797. The original Penn grant for this site is dated "25th of the 4th month, 1684 to Patrick Robinson." Robinson was a member of Council, Clerk of the Provincial Court, Register of Wills and a prominent merchant. In 1691 he sold the entire tract to another Quaker, Daniel Pegg. At that time the property was called Peterstone. In

11-See page 84

1696 Pegg sold the place to John Warner and it descended to several Warners until 1791 when John Ross bought it. It was during the Warner ownership that the fishing club known as the Colony in Schuykill rented a bank side area for their club house and headquarters.

Ross erected a small farm house there that same year. Samuel Breck, who had married the daughter of John Ross, next came into possession and built the handsome house which stands today, in 1797.

Samuel Breck was born in Boston in 1771. His father had been the fiscal agent of the French Forces in America during the Revolution and French Naval Officers were frequent guests in his house.

Through the influence of the Marquis de Vaudreuil, Samuel was sent to school in France for several years. He had grown to manhood by the time he arrived in Philadelphia, a fluent French scholar, gifted musician, artist, and interested in science; he wrote with a ready pen and delightful wit. Samuel married Jean Ross on Christmas Eve, 1795, and her father, John Ross, presented them with the property on the Schuylkill as a wedding present.

Ever hospitable and a genial host, Breck soon made Sweetbrier the gathering place for all the French, either in the diplomatic corps or visiting in Philadelphia including, of course, his old friend the Marquis de Lafayette. The Marquis wrote home of this visit, "the city was all alive, and a round of entertainments was kept up . . . a society of elegant and fashionable and stylish people."

Breck became a State Senator and a Congressman, a founder of the Savings Fund Society, and a Trustee of the University of Pennsylvania. One of Breck's particular interests was the Pennsylvania Institution for the Instruction of the Blind and he frequently entertained "his blind children" at Sweetbrier. Breck was also a member of the Macpherson Blues.

He loved Sweetbrier and took a tremendous interest in improving the place. In his "Recollections" he describes his home in detail, adding this charming account of the view: "The prospect consists of the river, animated by its great trade carried on in boats . . . drawn by horses; of a beautiful sloping lawn, terminating at the river, now nearly four hundred yards wide opposite the portico; of side-screen woods; of gardens, greenhouses, etc."

The estate also included an island in the river, and in 1819 Breck complained about the vandals and noisy groups which rowed out to the island and milked his cows. When the dam was built, Breck collected $5,139.60 from the City in 1823 for the destruction of the "wharf, still-house, stone wall and 16-3/4 acres," plus the aforesaid island which was submerged.

Samuel Breck died in 1862 having survived his wife by five years. He was 90 years of age. Whether his daily imbibing of five or six glasses of marsala wine prolonged his life is a moot question.

Breck had sold Sweetbrier to William S. Torr in 1838 and the City took possession in 1866.

In 1877 it was a restaurant and later a day camp for children. Finally the Junior League established it as their headquarters in 1927 and did considerable restoration. In 1939 the Junior League released Sweetbrier to the Modern Club who maintain it at present.

Sweetbrier is one of the first Philadelphia mansions to have long first floor windows, commonly called "French windows," and Breck probably derived this idea in architecture from his sojourn in France.

Sweetbrier is open to the public.[12]

CHAMOUNIX MANSION, MONTPELIER

IN 1677 some four hundred acres of this site was surveyed and called by the Indian name "Metoptum." It then belonged to John and Andreas Wheeler. After John's death the land was subdivided and sold to a succession of owners. The Roberts family were the longest owners, owning most of the property for nearly a hundred years. Thomas Mifflin, Governor of Pennsylvania, invested in a part at one time. In 1799 George Plumstead purchased 27 acres of this Mifflin tract.

George Plumstead came of a prominent Philadelphia family.

12-See page 84

Chamounix Mansion

His grandfather, Clement, and his father, William, had both been Mayors of the City. William serving for three terms, 1750, 1754, and 1756.

Clement Plumstead was an English Quaker and became a successful merchant in Philadelphia.

William inherited his father's property and business and like his father, married twice, his second wife being an Episcopalian, Mary McCall. She bore him seven children, of which George was the youngest and the only one to survive and marry.

George grew up in his family business, specializing in the India trade.

The Plumsteads purchased the tract which was to contain their mansion in 1799. By this time the old Indian name of Meptotum had been sophisticated to Montpelier. George built the house about 1800.

It is of Federal architecture and the entrance faced towards the river as the waterway was easier than the forest roads. George was not the successful merchant that his forebears had been and when he died in 1805 he left nothing but debts. Chamounix Mansion was sold at auction by T. B. Freeman, the ancestor of the present Samuel T. Freeman and Company, auctioneers, at the Merchants Coffee House.

The name Chamounix is supposed to be derived from a nearby pond of that name which has since been filled in.

Benjamin Johnson was the successful bidder for Chamounix Mansion and moved there from Ridgeland when Jacob Waln acquired the latter. The Johnson family occupied Chamounix for over a hundred years, during which time they added to it about 1856. The City took possession in 1871 and incorporated it in Fairmount Park. From 1887 it was a boarding house and restaurant from June to September, gradually deteriorating to only a refreshment stand with minimum repairs, and finally the abode of a Park Guard.

In 1963, with the cooperation of the Park Commission, the American Youth Hostels made extensive repairs and opened it to the public in 1964 as an International Youth Hostel.

Chamounix Mansion is the first City owned hostel in the United States and besides being a hostel serves as a meeting place for various community groups.

The stable, which is of Gothic revival architecture, is used as a recreation center for day camps.[13]

THE LILACS

THIS IS A farm house built in two contrasting sections. The earliest was a typical Pennsylvania farm house of the eighteenth century with a corner fireplace and adjacent staircase. The later section was added in 1832 by the Garrett family and is Federal in architecture and has a second story. The fireplaces have Adamesque mantels, and one has a composition of Franklin and Washington heads.

The house got its name from the wealth of lilac bushes which surrounded it. The children of the family used to cut bunches of lilacs and take them out to the River Road to sell to the carriage folks.

For many years The Lilacs was the up river boat house of the University Barge Club.

The oarsmen would row up the river from Boat House Row and leaving their shells on special stands, climb up the steps to their clubhouse for cooling libations and friendly chat. In the spring and fall, especially on moonlight nights, members gave "Barge Parties" and members with their invited lady guests, rowed

13-See page 84

up in a large barge which had an extra non-sliding seat beside each rower. On these occasions the oarsmen dressed in their official uniform which, for the University Barge Club, consisted of red shirts, with black binding and club insignia on the collars, and white trousers. The barge would be gay with the club flag at the bow and the American flag at the stern. One of the jobs of the cockswain, besides steering, was to try to keep the rowers in unison. The oars were so long that if a man became too interested in his fair companion and got out of time, he was liable to hit the man in front of him in the back. When such an event did happen it was taken good naturedly, but generally gave rise to pointed remarks. There was quite a ritual connected with the serving of the dinner when they arrived at The Lilacs. When everyone stood at his or her place at the table, the host gave the order "toss," at which each one stood their knives and forks on end, at the order "let fall," dropped them down with considerable clatter. Then everyone was seated. This custom, with various differentiations, was also observed at parties by other boat clubs who had up river houses.

After dinner there might be dancing to the music of a gramophone and then the row home by moonlight. The big decision to be made on the home trip was whether to go inside or outside the island just above the Belmont Offices. The passageway on the inside of the island is now filled in and the University Barge Club no longer maintains The Lilacs.

GREENLAND

IT was built about 1825 and adjacent to The Lilacs. Prior to 1807 the land was owned by Archibald Watson and was sold at Sheriff's sale in that year to John Warner. The next owner was Benjamin Johnson who seems to have been quite a developer and laid out the tract into what he called "The Village of Greenland." In 1836 Ralph McClintock bought some thirty-six acres of this tract including the Greenland Farm. The house was a substantial farm house which has been greatly altered and most of the original woodwork is gone.

The McClintocks had no children so a nephew, Leckey Murray Service, inherited the property and lived there with his family for a number of years.

Dr. Service was a graduate of Jefferson Medical College and became one of the leading practitioners, with patients in Philadelphia, Montgomery and Delaware Counties. He first started out from Greenland on his rounds, with his own medicines and on horseback. Later he attained a buggy, but still concocted his own prescriptions.

Eventually the estate came into the possession of Joshua B. Lippincott, founder of J. B. Lippincott and Company, through his wife, who was a niece of Mrs. Ralph McClintock.

Lippincott sold it to the City in 1869.

RIDGLAND, MOUNT PROSPECT

WILLIAM PENN deeded a large tract in 1684 to John Bowles and John Skutten.

In 1698 the tract was divided and the site of Ridgland went to John Skutten.

It was sold to William Couch who spoke in his will of 1762 of "my dwelling house and plantation."

The present house is accredited to Benjamin Johnson and dated about 1806. He called the place Mount Prospect. Jacob S. Waln bought part of the property in 1814 and added acreage in 1820. The Walns used it as a summer residence until Jacob's death in 1850. Waln changed the name of his home to Ridgland.

Jacob S. Waln served on the City Council and was a member of the Pennsylvania Legislature.

Ridgland was sold to the City in 1869 and is the official home of the Director of Fairmount Park.

It is not open to the public.

Belmont Mansion c.1747+   Fairmount Park

BELMONT MANSION

THIS PROPERTY had orginally been a large colonial planta-
of 442 acres of which Judge William Peters, brother of the
Reverend Doctor Richard Peters of Christ Church, purchased 220
acres, including Peter's Island in the river, in 1742. Judge Peters
made extensive alterations to the already existing house and added
more buildings from time to time.

William Peters became Register of the Admirality, Judge of
the Court of Common Pleas and a member of the State Legislature
from 1752 to 1756.

When the Revolution broke out Judge William Peters remained a Loyalist and returned to England, where he died.

His son, Richard, named after his uncle, stayed in America
and became an associator, member of the Continental Congress
and Pennsylvania Assembly, and during the Revolution served as
Commissioner of War. Richard became owner of Belmont Mansion
in 1786 and lived there until his death in 1828. He too became a
Judge of the U. S. District Court.

During Richard's occupancy Belmont Mansion was the scene
of much entertaining; the guests included most of the prominent
men and women of the Colonial and Federal era. Richard added
the beautiful plaster ceilings, ornamented with the family coat-
of-arms and devices representing musical instruments about 1790.

46

As time went on most of the surrounding property was whittled away, but fortunately the main house survived, although much deteriorated. What was left became part of Fairmount Park in 1867.

The house sits on a bluff with a magnificent view of the city, especially the lights at night. There is now a restaurant there and with its close proximity to the Playhouse in the Park, is very popular.

ADDENDUM #1

EAST BANK

PAGODA AND LABYRINTH GARDEN

A FANTASTIC Chinese Pagoda and Labyrinth Garden were erected in 1828, not far from the Fairmount Waterworks. The promoter was P. A. Browne and the building was designed by John Haviland.

The idea probably derived from the Oriental Pagoda at Kew. To add to its attraction, Chinese windbells were hung from projecting beams, but even their melodious beckoning was not alluring enough for the staid Quaker gentry of Philadelphia for according to Dr. George B. Tatum in *Penn's Great Town,* it was a failure from the beginning and closed the next year, but Mr. Harold D. Eberlein said in a *Portrait of a Colonial City* that it was very popular and lasted for ten years.

It really does not matter much for it no longer exists. There is a picture of the building and its surroundings in the Historical Society of Pennsylvania.

PHILADELPHIA MUSEUM OF ART

THIS IS one of the great museums of the world. It was designed by the firm of Charles L. Borie, Jr., Horace Trumbauer, and Clarence Zantzinger, and built on the old Faire Mount.

The building was started in 1919 and the first section was opened to the public in 1928. It is constructed of pure Minnesota dolomite and covers ten acres.

Besides works of art from all over the world dating from prehistoric to modern times, there are fifteen galleries devoted to Philadelphia furniture, silver, ceramics, etc. The Titus C. Geesey Collection of Pennsylvania German Arts, opened in 1958. The Charles Patterson Van Pelt Auditorium was opened in 1959 and the Great Hall completed in 1963. There are period rooms, a Japanese Tea House, a Japanese Buddhist Temple, a Catalan cloister, a French Gothic Chapel, a Chinese Buddhist Temple, and a Chinese scholar's study of the eighteenth century, to mention some of the treasures.

There are free guided tours.[14]

14-See page 85

THE RIVER

THE WATER AREA of the Schuylkill River within the Fairmount Park limits comprises some 379 acres. The name Schuylkill is supposed to derive from the old Dutch "hidden river" as the mouth where it enters the Delaware was so.hidden by rushes it was difficult to find.

At first the river was only used for transportation due to the thick forests on either side. The first boats were the Indian canoes, coming down to trade with the Swedes, then the batteau of the fur traders. After this the barges of the families with estates on the Hills and the fleets of the Fort St. Davids and Colony in Schuylkill fishing clubs.

Gradually as roads were opened and Philadelphians were more established, the river became a pleasure route as well.

A canal was constructed along the west bank in 1824 and a lock added when the dam was built so that boats could continue to the Delaware. This was destroyed when the Schuylkill Expressway was built. A small boat named the "Lady of the Lake" made the trip from Philadelphia to Reading in one day, the fare being $2.50 per person.

Between 1870 and 1890 steamers carrying fifty passengers ran up as far as the Falls, stopping at the various estate landings. During the Centennial Fair, 1876, the Fairmount Steamboat Company operated as many as a dozen boats.

On the east side of the river at Faire Mount was a tavern called the Rialto House which catered to the public who came to enjoy the waterworks, and became the headquarters of the sporting rowers until they formed into clubs and erected their own Boat House Row. There were other taverns along the east bank with a famous one at the Falls, owned by a widow named Blackwood who rented the house from Dr. William Smith in 1750 which is still in existence, although not as pristine as of yore. It was called the Old Falls Tavern.

In the early days there were few bridges across the river, but numerous fords and ferries. Dr. Smith was the proprietor of a ferry in connection with his tavern. It was operated by ropes which ran from shore to shore. The rules were that through traffic on the river had the right of way and the passage of the ferry was often impeded.

When the ferry was replaced by a chain bridge it enhanced the tavern business, for sightseers came up on the boats to see what was probably one of the earliest samples of a suspension bridge, and paused to indulge in fresh catfish and coffee at the nearby hostelry.

One of the pre-Revolutionary amenities were the two social fishing clubs on the banks of the river, Fort St. Davids by the Falls on the east bank and the Schuylkill Fishing Company of the Colony in Schuylkill on the west bank, on part of the Sweetbrier estate. Fort St. Davids, organized in 1747, had a club house called The Citadel in which congenial gentlemen of the surrounding estates and fishing enthusiasts met during the fishing season beginning the first of May and continuing every Friday during the season. Watson says, "much good living was enjoyed there," and that the walls were decorated with Indian relics. The fishing must have been excellent for the records state that the members caught and cooked forty catfish at a time, the other species being perch and rockfish. The caretaker for the club ran a shad fishery of his own on the side and recorded that he caught 430 fish in one haul. The Roberts family of Pencoyd had a fishery on the opposite side of the river.

Although the majority of the members remained Loyalists, the Hessians, in 1777-8, took the timbers of the club house with which to erect their huts. After the War the club was dissolved and the remaining members joined the Colony in Schuylkill.

The Schuylkill Fishing Company of the Colony was organized in 1748 as a gentlemen's fishing and hunting club. The first club house, called the Court House, was situated on the land belonging to a Quaker, William Warner, to whom the club paid a yearly rent of three fresh sunfish. This property eventually became part of the Sweetbrier estate.

After several removals the club still exists on the Delaware River and is the oldest English-speaking club in continuous existence in the world. After the Revolution the official name was changed from the Colony to the State in Schuylkill, but it is popularly known as "The Fish House."

Boat clubs with racing crews have replaced the fishing clubs and there is a public boat house where sailboats, canoes and rowboats can be rented, so that during the summer months the river presents an active scene, while hopeful fishermen line the banks.

Before the river became so polluted, there were gay skating parties in winter. Perhaps this may again be possible.

Most of the boat clubs are joined together in the Schuylkill Navy of Philadelphia.

THE SCHUYLKILL NAVY
OF PHILADELPHIA

THIS ORGANIZATION was started in 1858 and incorporated in 1882, and is the oldest amateur athletic governing body in America.

The object was to secure united action among the several clubs and to promote amateurism on the Schuylkill River.

It started with nine clubs and each club is represented by a senior and junior delegate which forms the Naval Board, headed by a Commodore. They staged their first official Regatta on the river in connection with the Centennial Exposition, 1876. It was an international affair with twenty-five organizations from all over the United States and a number of foreign countries participating.

The Navy is frequently asked to participate in municipal functions and on November 11, 1872, fourteen boats from various clubs formed an escort in the funeral solemnities for General George Meade. On April 27, 1878, they staged a demonstration in honor of a visit by President Rutherford B. Hayes to Philadelphia. In 1882 they held an Open Regatta in connection with the Bi-Centennial Celebration. In October, 1908, there was an Inter-City Regatta as part of the celebration of Founders Week and in 1937 they presented a huge Water Pageant for the celebration of the Constitution. One of the attractions was a Float depicting the signing of the Constitution in Independence Hall on a spot-lighted barge for a stage. It must have been a colorful event for besides the participants the river was filled with all sorts of spectator craft while thousands of people lined the banks. Boat House Row was decorated with bunting and flags and a band performed.

The Peoples' Regatta, which is held every 4th of July, is under the auspices of the Schuylkill Navy.

Early in the history of the Navy a Navy Review was held, usually in connection with the Annual Regatta. After going through various maneuvers the boats lined up across the river below the Girard Avenue Bridge for the Scrub Race, for which the Commodore awarded a trophy. An especially spectacular event for this race occured on June 2, 1935, when seventy-one boats of all kinds took part, with rowers of antiquity as well as present champions. It was climaxed by the Olympic Salute, when the river full of oarsmen held up their right arms simultaneously at the end.

There was so much traffic on the river that the Navy established the following rules:

1. All oarsmen in singles and crew must keep well to the east bank in going up river.
2. All oarsmen in singles and crews must keep well to the west side in coming down river.
3. All singles, or crews, going up river must STOP at Columbia Bridge and PROCEED CAUTIOUSLY on account of the possibility of races, or time trials coming down over the course.
4. All singles, or crews in races, time trials, or under test conditions coming over the course TAKE PRECEDENCE to all crews going up the river, and should be given the right of way.

   NOTE: Motor Boats, Canoes, etc., must also abide by the above rules, as there is great danger of accident if these regulations are not observed. Anyone violating these rules will, according to law, be held responsible for any personal and property damage resulting from collision.

Charles M. Prevost of the Camilla Barge Club was the first Commodore and the original clubs were: America, Camilla,

Chebucto, Falcon, Independent, Keystone, Neptune, Pennsylvania (not the University of), and University, also disconnected with the college. Soon afterwards the Nautilus, Quaker City, and Amateurs joined the Navy. Many of these clubs disbanded over the years or were absorbed by younger clubs. When the crews from the clubs compete against outside oarsmen they go with the backing of the Schuylkill Navy and they have sent winning crews to the Rowing Classics of the World.

For instance, among some of the outstanding victories were the following: in 1900 the Vesper 8-oared shell won the Olympics in Paris, France, and repeated the victory in 1904 in Toronto, Canada. In 1920 John B. Kelly of Vesper Boat Club was the first American to ever win the Single Sculls Olympic in Brussels, Belgium. The Schuylkill Navy presented him with the Philadelphia Challenge Cup which is for rowing what the Davis Cup is for tennis. It has been won by several foreign oarsmen as well as Americans. At that same Regatta, John B. Kelly and Paul Costello, also of Vesper, won the Double Sculls Race. They won again in 1924 in Paris, this time representing the Penn Athletic Club Rowing Association. In 1922 Walter M. Hoover of the Undine Barge Club won the English Diamond Sculls. 1930 the 8-oared shell of the Penn Athletic Club Rowing Association won the International Championship at the Regatta in Liege, Belgium, defeating eight other countries. In 1932 W. E. Garrett Gilmore and Kenneth Myers of the Bachelors Barge Club won the Double Sculls at the Olympic at Long Beach, California, and the Pair-Oared Shells Race with Coxswain was won by Charles M. Kieffer and Joseph A. Schauers with Coxswain Edward F. Jennings. This was the first time an American crew won a race in this class.

The official Henley Course on the river was inaugurated about 1901 or 1902 through the efforts of the University Barge Club. The American Henley Regatta races alternate each year between Philadelphia and Boston.

In 1935 the Navy started Match Races on Saturday afternoons during the summer, limited to the clubs belonging to the Navy. These proved so popular they were continued. School Boy Crews were organized by Penn Charter in 1898. They were coached by

James Bond, the coach of the Bachelors Barge Club and student of the famous Ellis Ward, while the University Barge Club lent them the shells. W. E. Garrett Gilmore, the founder of organized schoolboy rowing, knew whereof he spoke for he had won eighteen American and seven Canadian Championships and was a Captain, i.e., President of the Bachelors Barge Club and Commodore of the Schuylkill Navy.

The boys have made good. The Lower Merion High School crew won the schoolboy Junior eight oar championship of the United States in Washington, D. C., in 1952 and other schools have made records since. The Schoolboy Rowing Association of America Regatta is open to any crews of any public or private school given to the education of youth.

On Regatta Day, no individual entered in senior events may be over 19 years, 6 months of age and for the junior events 17 years, 6 months. Besides rowing races on the Schuylkill River, schoolboy crews belonging to the Association compete in such places as Massachusetts, Princeton, New Jersey, Detroit, Arlington, Buffalo, Poughkeepsie, New York, with frequent Philadelphia winners.

In 1927 Mr. Edward T. Stotesbury, a member of the Bachelors Barge Club, presented a cup for the junior 8-oared shells with individual medals for the crew.

Among the many cups and trophies awarded for all these races perhaps the first Philadelphia one was offered by J. E. Caldwell and Company in 1888, "for the encouragement of rowing as a pasttime and to promote closer competition among the several clubs of the Navy."

The present membership of the Schuylkill Navy consists of Commodore Joseph J. Sonzogni and the following clubs: Bachelors Barge Club, College Boat Club, Crescent Boat Club, Fairmount Rowing Association, Malta Boat Club, Penn Athletic Club Rowing Association, Undine Barge Club, University Barge Club, and Vesper Boat Club.

BOAT HOUSE ROW

IN 1853 the present site of Boat House Row was an industrial area with the river front a series of docks and piers. Rolling mills, marine facturing plants and taverns occupied much of what is today the East River Drive, extending up to the Girard Avenue Bridge.

When the clubs decided to have homes of their own they erected wooden shacks in which to keep their equipment. These were so fragile they were quickly subject to vandalism. The Bachelors relate that when their shack was robbed of their uniforms and flags, the members armed themselves and went on a round of the nearby taverns, with the successful recovery of most of their property. As soon as the clubs could gather the money they built the handsome, substantial club houses of today. The first building of Boat House Row is Plaisted Hall, named after a prominent rower. The structure originally contained a carrousel and refreshment parlor; boats could also be rented from there. It is probably on the site of one of the old taverns. The merry-go-round part has been turned into a basketball court since 1947 under the Department of Recreation and there is a small concession at the other end where ice cream and cakes can be purchased.

The original racing boats had stationary seats and the oarsman sewed a patch of leather or chamois to the seat of his pants to which he added a heavy coat of grease, allowing him to slide on the seat. Sliding seats did not come in until about 1876.

Gradually the clubs adopted two sets of costume, one for dress in the parades or when they gave barge parties, and the other for racing. The original formal garb was white Navy blouses with wide turned down collars, flapping bell-bottom trousers of white canvas, blue pea jackets with brass buttons, fancy colored waistcoats or gay belts of satin or silk, generally of that particular boat club colors, broad-brimmed sailor hats with fluttering ribbons also of the club colors and polished pumps. For racing they wore jerseys or T shirts of the club colors, short trousers and sneakers. The blades of the oars were also painted with the club colors.

Besides the various types of racing shells, most of the clubs had working boats for practice, barges for heavy duty and parties, with such delightful names as "Iris, of the Philadelphia Barge Club," "Ione, of the Crescent," "Thistle, of the Quaker City Club," and "Linda, of the Bachelors."

Iris was painted green with a gold stripe running around it just below the gunwale, Ione was painted red with a similar gold stripe. When in action all barges had an American flag at the stern and the club pennant at the bow.

Some of the clubs had up river houses where they could relax and give parties and when there is a Regatta on, all the boat houses on Boat House Row are decorated with their flags and bunting.

All the clubs own their club houses. Practically all the clubs in the Row have ancient history and their shelves are filled with trophies.

The Bachelors Barge Club was organized in 1853 and their up river house is still in existence, appropriately called "The Button."

The College Boat Club was organized in 1872.

The Crescent Boat Club dates from 1867.

The Fairmount Rowing Association started in 1877.

The Malta Boat Club has an especially interesting background. It was founded in 1860 and originally rowed on the Delaware River, moving to the Schuylkill in 1865 where they first used a place called Pop's Boat House and then the old club house of the extinct Excelsior Boat Club, finally erecting their present home.

The Malta was founded by the Minniehaha Lodge of an old organization called the Sons of Malta who claimed to have a charter from the Knights of Malta. The Sons of Malta had quite a few chapters both in the north and in the south which were dissolved by the Civil War and so far as is known the Malta Boat Club is their only surviving organization.

The Penn Athletic Club Rowing Association is a comparatively new comer having been organized in 1925.

The Undine Barge Club was organized in 1856 and still has an up river club house.

The University Barge Club, which has nothing to do with the University of Pennsylvania, was organized in 1854. They had The Lilacs for their up river club house and in 1932 absorbed the Philadelphia Barge Club which had the Anchorage, now a public restaurant.

The Vesper Boat Club started in 1865.

There are two womens' organizations on Boat House Row: The Philadelphia Girls Rowing Club, started by Mrs. Ernie Bayer, wife of the Olympic sculler, in 1938. They occupy and own the building once the headquarters of the Philadelphia Skating Club and Humane Society. The latter group was formed when skating was a popular sport on the river and the members were pledged to go to the rescue of anyone falling through the ice. All members were supposed to be equipped with a coil of rope for emergencies.

And the Sedgley Club. This club occupies a building which includes the lighthouse, originally warning river traffic of the dam. The lighthouse was built by the City in the early eighteen hundreds as a beacon for the steamers plying the River. Traffic continuing down to the Delaware River would here enter a lock and be transported around the dam. The lock was filled in when the Schuylkill expressway was constructed.

The Sedgeley Club was organized in 1897 as a Ladies' Rowing Club, under the guiding spirit of Miss Madge L. Corlies and at first shared the Philadelphia Skating Club house. In February

1902 they applied to the Fairmount Park Commission for permission to erect their own club house, but the Park Commission refused as, they said, there were too many clubs already. Nothing daunted, the Ladies put pressure on their spouses and other diplomatic channels and eventually the Commission yielded and the site by the lighthouse was chosen. On December 11, 1902, ground was broken with a gala ceremony. The officers and board of the Club consisting of Miss Corlies, *President*, Mrs. Lucretia Stevens Heckscher, *Secretary*, Mrs. Eli K. Price, *Treasurer*, and the Board of Mrs. Frederick A. Packard, Miss Christine Biddle, Mrs. R. H. Bayard Bowie, Mrs. C. Leland Harrison, Mrs. J. Willis Martin, Miss Mary Keating and Miss Mary Large brandished spades, while the other members of the club sported paddles with "Sedgley" painted on the blades. After which there was a board meeting and tea.

Arthur H. Brockie was the architect and he cleverly incorporated the lighthouse in his design. It is the first women's club house in the Park. For a number of years a row boat and landing stage was maintained for the convenience of the members, but gradually the club turned to more social activities, installing a piano, pianola, ping pong table, quoits, and bean bags. Luncheons, costing 50 cents per member, were cooked by the member caterer of the day. Today the Club is used for luncheons and bridge with professional caterers, or parties given by the members. The lighthouse no longer guides shipping, but remains an interesting landmark.

In the college world the University of Pennsylvania occupies its own house and in June, 1967, the varsity oarsmen won the Intercollegiate Rowing Association Championship, bringing it to Pennsylvania for the first time in 67 years.

Further up the river, the Strawberry Mansion Canoe House is a public boat house where several types of craft can be rented and the berth of the Sun Fish fleet. The Temple University crews use it as their headquarters. It is a very popular spot and bus loads of water-minded young and old come for a day's outing when as many as nineteen canoes are taken out at once. Refreshments can also be had here.

64

POWELTON

THIS TRACT belonged to Thomas Willing and Tench Francis. In 1775 Samuel Powel and his wife, Elizabeth Willing Powel, purchased 97 acres for a summer home. Here they built a house about 1779. Supposedly it was not a very elaborate mansion, but, as both Mr. and Mrs. Powel were cultured people and their town house today is one of the handsomest in Society Hill, they doubtless erected a gentleman's abode. Samuel Powel had lived in Europe for quite a while and his wife came from one of Philadelphia's most distinguished families.

As the Mayor of Philadelphia under the Provincial Government and the first Mayor under the Republican rule, Powel would have had to do considerable entertaining, so his country seat, which he called Powelton, would have to be more than a glorified farm house. In fact there is a record that President Washington attended a gathering of the Sons of Tammany there.

Samuel Powel died at Powelton in 1793 of the yellow fever. There is no record as to the fate of this house, but in 1800 Mrs. Powel began a new house also called Powelton, on what she called the Powelton Farm. This is supposed to be the center of the final creation by John Hare Powel, her nephew and inheritor of the family fortune. John Hare Powel had also traveled extensively and was a prominant art collector and connoisseur, who fancied his own architectural abilities and had a passion for building. In fact he built three very handsome houses in various parts of Philadelphia over a period of years.

In his youth John Hare Powel was a Brigade Major of the Washington Guards during the War of 1812 and later Inspector General with the rank of Colonel in the Regular Army. John Hare Powel added wings and a portico to Powelton House between 1825 and 1826. It was considered the earliest example of a private country house in the Philadelphia area to use the Greek Revival architecture. William Strickland had something to do with the design, but John Hare Powel had such an exalted opinion of his own architectural creations he frequently wore out the patience of his architects. Powel never finished Powelton and sold the estate to the Pennsylvania Railroad Company in 1851. The Railroad only wanted the lowlands on which to run their tracks so parted with the remaining 63 acres, which included the house on the higher ground, for residential development.

In 1860 E. Spencer Miller, whose wife was a Hare, bought Powelton and two acres of the surrounding land. The Millers completed the building and furnishings and lived there until 1883.

By this time so-called progress and industry was crowding so, they disposed of the property to the firm of Wendell and Smith who demolished the house in 1885, cut streets through the site and built small row houses which they called Powelton Village.

Grant's Cabin

GRANT'S CABIN

THE CABIN was built in 1864 on a bluff overlooking the James River at City Point, Va., and occupied by General U. S. Grant, Commander-in-Chief of the Union Armies as his headquarters from November, 1864 to March 29, 1865.

In this cabin Grant wrote the order to General Sherman for his march through the Carolinas, and the order to General Sheridan, summoning him to the Army of the Potomac for the final struggle.

The cabin contains two rooms and Mrs. Grant spent most of the winter there with him. Lincoln, Meade and most of the other Union Generals consulted Grant in this little house. Here he received the Confederate Commissioners who came from Richmond to treat for the peace in March, 1865, and finally he wrote the orders for the concluding operations of the War, reported to Lincoln before the Armies started on the campaign that ended at Appomattox and Lee's surrender.

At the close of the War, General Grant presented the cabin to George H. Stuart, then President of the Sanitary Commission, and Mr. Stuart's heirs presented the cabin to the City of Philadelphia in 1898. It was placed in Fairmount Park about fifty yards from the remains of the breast-works thrown up by the Pennsylvania Home Guard during the Battle of Gettysburg, for the Union Army to fall back to in case they were defeated.

The tablet marking the cabin was contributed by the Dames of the Loyal Legion Society of the State of Pennsylvania and affixed in 1922.

SMITH'S MEMORIAL PLAY GROUNDS

THE CHILDREN'S PLAYHOUSE AND PLAYGROUNDS

THESE WERE FOUNDED and maintained under the wills of Richard and Sarah A. Smith.

The building was designed by James H. Windrum and is in memory of the Smith's only son, Stanfield Smith.

Richard Smith was a member of the firm of MacKeller, Smith and Jordan—type founders. He died in 1894 and in his will left

$50,000 for a building and playground for children in the Park. Mrs. Smith died in 1895 and left her estate towards the equipment and maintenance.

The building is beautifully equipped for indoor games and story telling in the winter. There is a dispensary and registered nurse for minor accidents, facilities for keeping baby foods on ice and a kitchen for heating them.

The place was opened to the public July 23, 1899.

ROBIN HOOD DELL

ROBIN HOOD DELL is a natural amphitheater and is considered acoustically one of the finest outdoor "concert halls" in America.

It can accommodate more than 20,000 people. The first concert was given July 8, 1930.

Free tickets are distributed by the Department of Recreation through coupons in the daily newspapers.

Concerts are held, weather permitting, Mondays, Tuesdays and Thursdays during the summer months, beginning at 8:00 P. M.

The concerts are held under the auspices of the Philadelphia Plan of the City Council and financially assisted by Friends of the Dell. Nearly all the great artists of the world have performed at the Dell, including, of course, the Philadelphia Orchestra.

The Dell derives its name from its proximity to the old Robin Hood Ford and the Robin Hood Tavern which stood on the Ridge Road near Heart Lane.

LAUREL HILL CEMETERY

THE CEMETERY was created from three estates in 1836.

North Laurel Hill from the estate of Joseph Sims, known as Laurel; Central Laurel Hill from the site of George Pepper's estate, known as Fairy Hill; and South Laurel Hill from the site of William Rawle's estate, known as Harleigh.

68

The cemetery grounds were designed by John Notman and for many years it was a popular place for Philadelphians to come for a stroll or a day's outing.

FOUNTAIN GREEN

IN 1778 General Thomas Mifflin purchased a tract at the Falls of the Schuylkill from Sarah Lewis. The deed describes it as containing a "Messuage or Tenement and Two Tracts . . . of Land."

As Governor of Pennsylvania, Mifflin had to have a rather elaborate home and he spent plenty of money on improvements.

Besides being Governor of the Commonwealth, Mifflin had been Quartermaster General of the Patriot Armies in the Revolution and President of the Continental Congress.

When the property was offered for sale in 1833, the advertisement listed a "splendid mansion, gardener's house, ice house, milk house, bath house for warm, cold, and shower bathing, carriage house and stables, and general farm equipment." Special mention was made that water was piped into the house—no more going to the well.

When Andrew McMackin became the owner in 1840 he added another novelty, a coal furnace.

All these magnificent appointments have been absorbed by the industrial march around the Falls, and are no more.

SMITH'S OCTAGON, SMITH'S FOLLY

DR. WILLIAM SMITH began purchasing land at the Falls of the Schuylkill in 1750. He built a house of original design known as "Smith's Octagon" which was known to be in existence by 1762. He purchased this tract from the Robeson's of Shoomac Park.

Dr. Smith was a native of Scotland and the first provost of the College, Academy and Charitable School of Philadelphia, later to become the University of Pennsylvania.

Dr. Smith established a ferry across the river just below the Falls and leased a house on his property to the widow Blackwood for a tavern, known as the Old Falls Tavern and still in existence, although somewhat changed in character.

Dr. Smith was a combative character who did not hesitate to raise his voice, especially against the Quakers. At one time he was cast into jail for some of his actions, but continued to hold his classes as usual amidst these dreary surroundings. He continued as head of the college until after the Revolution when, owing to his Loyalist activities, the Assembly banished him and he retired to Chestertown, Maryland. His properties were confiscated and like most of that area, the Octagon house succumbed to encroaching industry.

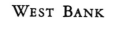

WEST BANK

THOMAS MOORE'S COTTAGE,
PIG-EYE COTTAGE

A SMALL COTTAGE built about 1805 on part of what is now the Belmont Offices of the Park. It is very similar in architecture to the Caleb Pusey House built in 1683.

It was supposed to have been occupied by the Irish poet, Thomas Moore, in 1804, but as he was in Philadelphia in 1804, before the house was built, and only remained in this country for ten days, when he was constantly wined and dined, a journey back and forth from Belmont to the city would have been a chore even if there was a house. But the name lingers.

For a tiny cottage, it has had more names than any of the dignified mansions.

It was first called "Pig-Eye Cottage" on account of its two small windows, in 1815. Then "Aunt Cornelia's Cottage" after a Negro tenant who lived there in 1849 and finally just plain "Belmont Cottage."

The whole complex of the Belmont offices are situated on part of the original Belmont plantation of which Belmont Mansion is the crowning star.

73

MEMORIAL HALL

MEMORIAL HALL was one of the few buildings purposely erected for permanency in connection with the Centennial Exposition, 1876.

It was designed by Hermann Joseph Schwarzmann as the Art Gallery for the Exposition, and called The Pennsylvania State Centennial Building. When the Exposition closed the building was presented, with all its contents, to the State and the City of Philadelphia.

The Pennsylvania Museum and School of Industrial Art was put in charge and the exhibits augmented by additions from the Park Commission, especially the Wilstach Collection. When the present Museum of Art was built on Faire Mount all the collections were transferred to the new building, and the main part of Memorial Hall was altered to house public indoor sports. Plans have been completed for offices in one of the wings for the Park Administration, now in the Belmont offices. This will centralize and modernize all the Park business and personnel, as well as provide a headquarters for the Park Guards, and be a vast improvement.

HORTICULTURAL HALL,
LANSDOWNE HOUSE

HORTICULTURAL HALL was another of the buildings erected in connection with the Centennial Exposition of 1876. It, too, was designed by Hermann Joseph Schwarzmann and was dedicated to the display of exotic plants.

The architecture was considered Moorish of the 12th century. Horticultural Hall continued to function until well into the 20th century, but finally became too ancient for costly repairs and was torn down in 1955.

Horticultural Hall was on the site of Lansdowne House.

Lansdowne House

John Penn, grandson of the Proprietor and cousin of John Penn of Solitude purchased a tract from William Smith of 140 acres between Belmont and the Warner (Sweetbrier) properties three years before the Revolution and erected a stately mansion. This John Penn was twice Governor of Pennsylvania Province.

Governor Penn married Ann Allen, daughter of Chief Justice Allen and, although deprived of his possessions by the War, was allowed to remain at Lansdowne House until his death in 1795. Mrs. Penn then sold to James Greenleaf, the partner of Robert Morris of the Hills, but their failure forced him to sell Lansdowne and it was purchased by the fabulously wealthy William Bingham in 1796.

The Binghams entertained royally there. When their daughter married Alexander Baring, later Lord Ashburton, Bingham built a house for them down near the river bank called The Hut. At this time Bingham was United States Senator from Pennsylvania.

After the Battle of Waterloo, Joseph Bonaparte, former King of Spain, rented the main house for a time.

After the Civil War the Baring descendants offered to sell the entire tract to the City for park purposes. On July 4, 1854 Lansdowne House was set on fire by fireworks and so badly damaged it had to be demolished.

During the British occupation of Philadelphia in 1777 they had an outpost stationed on the Lansdowne Estate.

JAPANESE TEMPLE GATE

JUST BELOW Horticultural Hall was a Japanese Temple Gate. It was presented to the City through the Fairmount Park Art Association by John H. Converse and Samuel W. Vauclain in 1905. The structure had formed part of the official Japanese exhibit at the Louisiana Purchase Exposition in St. Louis in 1904. The architecture was of three hundred years ago.

The gate and its contents, consisting of Japanese Art in wood, metal, and fabrics, were all purchased by Messrs. Converse and Vauclain. The contents were given to the Pennsylvania Museum and School of Industrial Art to be placed in Memorial Hall with the rest of their exhibits, and were later transferred to the present Art Museum. The usual Temple Guardians, Brahma and Indra were retained and placed at the entrance of the gate.

The gardens surrounding the Gate were donated by John H. Converse and John T. Morris and designed by Mr. Y. Muto, a Japanese Landscape Architect.

The Gate was burned to the ground on May 6, 1955.

ZOOLOGICAL GARDENS

THE ZOOLOGICAL SOCIETY of Philadelphia was incorporated 1859. Council allotted the land through the Park Commission to the Society in 1873.

The gardens are situated on the tract known as Solitude, and the grounds were laid out by Hermann J. Schwarzmann.

The main entrance pavilions were designed by Furness and Hewitt and built in 1873-75.

Furness also designed the first elephant house which has since been demolished and Hewitt designed the antelope house which still remains with some alterations. The present elephant house was designed by Paul Crêt, as well as the service buildings.

Through the generosity of Charles B. Penrose the Penrose Research Laboratory was established in 1901. It was the first of its kind in the world exclusively devoted to the study of wild animal pathology, and the main collection of animals created the first zoo in America. Other buildings were added designed by Edwin H. Clark with funds provided by the Catherwood, Chapman and Baker Funds.

The gardens were opened to the public in 1874.

The Daniel W. Dietrich Memorial Children's Zoo was opened in 1957. It is within the gardens.[15]

The Zoo is open from 10:00 A. M. to 5:00 P. M., and closed Thanksgiving, Christmas and New Year's Days.

JAPANESE EXHIBITION HOUSE

IT WAS presented in 1955 to the United States by the America-Japan Society, Tokyo, on behalf of the people of Japan, and sponsored by private citizens in Japan and the United States, and the Museum of Modern Art in New York. It was first placed in the garden of the Modern Museum, but in 1957 it was given to the Fairmount Park Commission for the City and re-erected in Fairmount Park. The Park Commission made a substantial contribution towards the cost of this work.

15-See page 85

77

The house was designed by Junzo Yoshimura and made in Nagoya in 1953.

The wood used in the construction of the main building is hinoki, a species of Japanese cypress, while the shingles on the roof were made of its bark. The house is a copy of a 16th and 17th century prototype which would have been constructed for a government official or a priest.

The surrounding garden was designed by Tansai Sano in consultation with David E. Engel.

Open to the public.

SHEEP FOLD

AT ONE TIME the Park Commission experimented with keeping flocks of sheep with the idea that they would save cutting large areas of grass.

The flocks were used mostly along the Chamounix Drive and a sheep fold and barn were erected close to Ridgland.

Power motors have since been introduced and the sheep barn has been converted into dressing rooms for the actors participating in the Playhouse in the Park.

GREENHOUSE AND NURSERIES

THE GREENHOUSE, located near the Horticultural Hall site under the very cooperative management of Charles Mathews, raises some 60,000 annual and potted plants yearly for various city offices, the concourse in the Municipal Services Building, Robin Hood Dell, Rittenhouse Square Easter Show, and the Flower Market, the Annual Spring Flower Show, floral decorations on City Department's floats used in civic parades and other civic requests, as well as supplying the various parks under the auspices of the Park Commission. It is a large order which is remarkably well carried out by a limited and highly skilled staff.

The Nurseries are on part of the old Greenland plantation. Here many hundreds of shrubs and trees of all varieties and sizes, ranging from common garden to specimens of rarity and unusual beauty provide plantings and replacements for the parks in general, Park Houses, John B. Kelly Playhouse and Pool, Art Museum, Rodin Museum, Landscaping of City Department's new facilities, such as the Police and Fire Departments, the Recreation Department, and the Street Tree programs which cover all the city streets.

The year round activities of the Greenhouse and Nurseries are among the major functions of the Fairmount Park, and contribute mightily to the beauty of the whole city as well as the parks.

PARK TROLLEYS

IN 1889 William Wharton, Jr., was licensed to run a Gravity Passenger Railway in Fairmount Park to take passengers to the major points of interest. The contract permitted him to construct, operate and maintain his investment for a period of fifty years, subject to the approval of the Park Commission. A quotation from this contract reads: "Article 5—Unless the express consent of the Park Commissioners, given in writing, the motive power of the said passenger railway shall be limited to electricity, cable traction, and the force of gravity upon the incline plane. At the end of 50 years the license may be continued for a further period of 10 years."

The official title was the Fairmount Park Transportation Company, and the road was built during 1896-97.

79

The Park trolleys were abolished September 9, 1946 and the car barn is now a storage and repair shop.

One of the happiest memories of old-timers still living are those rides on the Park trolleys. The cars were of the open type and only ran during the summer months. Whole families went for a day's outing, while the back seats were generally monopolized by loving couples. Until automobiles became general, a Park trolley ride was one of the most popular uses of the Park.

PARK HOUSE TOURS

The Fairmount Park House Tours Department of the Philadelphia Museum of Art was established in 1960 by the Women's Committee of the Museum. It has grown from seven professional guides to thirty-five, including several bi-lingual guides. They are trained under the auspices of the Museum in history, architecture, and decorative arts, and conduct tours for private groups, school classes, conventions, and "off the street" tourists. From one to 200 people can be accommodated simultaneously, with no more than 25 people to each guide.

On the tour agenda are selections from the six furnished eighteenth century houses in the park, the Japanese House, and Memorial Hall. As more houses are opened as museum houses, they will be included. In addition, the guides conduct walking tours through the Society Hill area of Philadelphia, comparing eighteenth century town and country life styles.

For tours and current information about hours and days the houses are open to the public, call the Fairmount Park House Tours Department of the Philadelphia Museum of Art, PO 3-8100, ext. 304.

SUMMARY

THIS BOOK is intended as a reference book of buildings and beings which cast a light upon the River Schuylkill, in Fairmount Park. No attempt has been made to record the history of that fine organization of Park Guards who contribute so much to the peace of the Park or the numerous fountains and statuary which enhance Fairmount.

Some of the contents relate to ancient times and others to a more modern era.

The object of these accounts is to try to inform the public of many aspects with which they are probably not familiar and instill in them an appreciation and pride in this unique and wonderful asset of the City of Philadelphia.

I have sincerely tried to be accurate, sifting out and cross-checking many divergent statements and records, as well as making personal visits. It has been a labor of love.

MARION W. RIVINUS

Chestnut Hill
1967

ADDENDUM #2

Footnote References

1. Fairmount Park is listed in the National Register of Historic Places of the United States Department of the Interior.

2. The waterworks buildings, now unoccupied, are part of a restoration project being undertaken by the Fairmount Park Commissioners.

3. An application to place Lemon Hill in the National Register of Historic Places is on file in the Philadelphia Historical Commission, the Pennsylvania Historical and Museum Commission, Harrisburg, and the United States Department of the Interior, Washington, D. C.

4. The Fairmount Park Art Association was organized in 1872 with the objectives of "adorning Fairmount Park, the streets, avenues, parkways, and public places in the City of Philadelphia with statues, busts, and other works of art, either of a memorial nature or otherwise; and to promote and foster the beautiful in the City of Philadelphia, in its architecture, improvements, and general plan."

   The earliest statue placed in the Park is of Major General George Gordon Meade by the elder Alexander Milne Calder, October 18, 1887. It is cast of 50 bronze cannon given by the United States Congress.

   Among other statues also placed in the Park are, Thortinn Karlsetni by Einar Jonsson, depicting a Norse Viking discoverer of America, The Medicine Man by Cyrus E. Dallin, of a mounted Indian and a Cowboy by Frederick Remington.

   The current project of the Association is compiling a book on the public sculpture in the City.

   The present offices of the Association is in the Philadelphia Museum of Art.

5. An application to place Strawberry Mansion in the National Register of Historic Places is on file in the Philadelphia Historical Commission, the Pennsylvania Historical and Museum Commission, Harrisburg, and the United States Department of the Interior, Washington, D. C.

6. Woodford is administered by the Trustees of the Naomi Wood Estate.

7. Rockland is under the auspices of the Delaware Valley Council of the American Youth Hostels and is their Service Program Headquarters. The facilities of the mansion are available to organizations holding A. Y. H. passes and all A. Y. H. Clubs.

8. Mount Pleasant is administered by the Philadelphia Museum of Art and is listed in the National Register of Historic Places.

9. Solitude is now maintained as one of the Zoological Garden buildings.

10. Elizabeth Coates Paschall purchased the land in 1746.

11. Cedar Grove is administered by the Philadelphia Museum of Art and an application to place it in the National Register of Historic Places is on file in the Philadelphia Historical Commission, the Pennsylvania Historical and Museum Commission, Harrisburg, and the United States Department of the Interior, Washington, D. C.

12. An application to place Sweetbrier in the National Register of Historic Places is on file in the Philadelphia Historical Commission, the Pennsylvania Historical and Museum Commission, Harrisburg and the United States Department of the Interior, Washington, D. C.

13. And has now been added to the equipment for hostelers in Chamounix Mansion.

14. An application to place the Museum of Art in the National Register of Historic Places is on file in the Philadelphia Historical Commission, the Pennsylvania Historical and Museum Commission, Harrisburg, and the United States Department of the Interior, Washington, D. C.

There are free guided tours conducted daily by the Volunteer Guides and special Gallery Talks and lectures by the Staff of the Division of Education. For current information call the Philadelphia Museum of Art, PO 3-8100.

15. An elevated monorail installed in 1969 traverses the Zoo, above the cages and gardens. It is the first of its kind in the Philadelphia area and the first monorail in any public Zoo in the world.

EAST BANK

1. Philadelphia Museum of Art
2. Fairmount Water Works
3. Boat House Row
4. Lemon Hill
5. Grant's Cabin
6. Hatfield House
7. The Cliffs
8. Mount Pleasant
9. Rockland
10. Ormiston
11. Randolph Mansion
12. Woodford
13. Strawberry Mansion

WEST BANK

14. The Solitude
15. Zoological Gardens
16. Letitia Street House
17. Sweetbrier
18. Cedar Grove
19. Memorial Hall
20. Japanese Exhibition House
21. Belmont Mansion
22. Sheep Fold and Barn
23. Ridgland
24. Chamounix Mansion
25. The Lilacs
26. Greenland
27. Thomas Moore's Cottage and Belmont offices of the Fairmount Park Commission.